COMMUNISM:

Effects and impacts on the country involved

Alexander J. Arnold

Table of Contents

Chapter 1: Communism, and the things to know about it

History of Communism

While the word communism was not generally used until the 1840s, civilizations that may be deemed communist were described as early as the 4th century BCE by the Greek philosopher Plato. In his Socratic dialogue Republic, Plato depicts an ideal society in which a governing class of guardians—mainly philosophers and soldiers—serves the interests of the entire community. Because individual ownership of property would make them self-seeking, indulgent, greedy, and corrupt, the governing guardians, Plato reasoned, had to act as a huge communal family that ownership of all material assets, as well as wives and children.

Religion influenced other early ideals of communism. In the Bible's Book of Acts, for example, the earliest Christians embraced a primitive sort of communism as both a method of sustaining unity and of avoiding the ills connected with the private ownership of worldly things. In several early monastic orders, the monks made vows of poverty forcing them to share their limited worldly things solely with one another and with the needy. In his futuristic 1516 essay Utopia, English politician Sir Thomas More depicts an ideally perfect society in which money is eliminated and the people share food, housing, and other commodities.

Contemporary communism was inspired in Western Europe by the Industrial Revolution of the late 18th and early 19th centuries. The revolution, which allowed some to attain great wealth at the expense of an increasingly impoverished working class, encouraged Prussian political activist, Karl Marx, to conclude that class struggles resulting from income inequality would inevitably give rise to a society in common ownership of the means of production would allow prosperity to be shared by all.

In 1848, Marx, together with German economist Friedrich Engels, produced The Communist Manifesto, in which they decided that the issues of poverty, sickness, and shorter lives that affected the proletariat—the working class—could be overcome only by replacing capitalism with communism. Under communism, as envisioned by Marx and Engels, the principal means of economic production—factories, mills, mines, and railroads—would be publicly owned and managed for the benefit of everyone.

Marx predicted that a fully realized form of communism following the overthrow of capitalism would result in a communal society free of class divisions or government, in which the production and distribution of goods would be based upon the principle "From each according to his ability, to each according to his needs." His numerous followers, notably Russian revolutionary Vladimir Lenin accepted Marx's ideals of a communist society.

During World War II, the Soviet Union collaborated with other European communist and socialist governments in resisting the fascist danger presented by Nazi Germany. However, the conclusion of the war also broke the already unstable alliance between the Soviet Union and its more politically moderate Warsaw Pact satellite nations, enabling the USSR to create communist governments throughout Eastern Europe.

The Russian Revolution of 1917 led to the founding of the Union of Soviet Socialist Republics (USSR) under Vladimir Lenin in 1922. By the 1930s, Lenin's brand of moderate communism had been superseded by the Communist Party of the Soviet Union, which under Joseph Stalin, established ultimate government control over all elements of the Russian society. Despite the incalculable human cost of his iron-fisted, authoritarian application of communism, Stalin transformed the Soviet Union from a backward country into a world superpower.

After the Second World War, the political tensions of the Cold War and the economic drain of maintaining its status as a global military superpower slowly weakened the Soviet Union's grip over its Eastern Bloc communist satellite nations, such as East Germany and Poland. By the 1990s, the prevalence of communism as a global political force quickly diminished. Today, only the nations of China, Cuba, North Korea, Laos, and Vietnam continue to function as communist states.

Communism is a form of government most frequently associated with the ideas of Karl Marx, a German philosopher who outlined his ideas for a utopian (ideal and perfect) society in The Communist Manifesto, written in 1848. Marx thought that capitalism, with its concentration on profit and private ownership, led to inequality among people. Thus, his purpose was to support a system that encouraged a classless society in which everyone shared the fruits of work and the state government controlled all property and money. No one would aspire to advance over others, and people would no longer be driven by greed. Then, communism would reduce the gap between wealthy and poor, stop the exploitation of labor, and liberate the poor from tyranny.

The essential principles of communism did not originate with Marx, however. Plato and Aristotle discussed them in ancient times, but Marx transformed them into a popular ideology, which was subsequently driven into practice. Marx's ideal society secured economic equality and justice. Marx thought that private ownership of property increased greed, and he blamed capitalism for society's ills. The issues, he said, arose from the Industrial Revolution. The emergence of factories, the dependence on machines, and the potential of mass production generated circumstances that supported oppression and favored the creation of a proletariat, or a working class.

Simply defined, under a capitalist system, the manufacturers fuelled the economy, and a rich minority owned the factories. This produced the need for a huge number of employees to work for the factory owners. In this climate, the privileged few exploited the proletariat, who had to labor to exist. So, Marx articulated his plan to liberate the proletariat or to relieve them of the burden of work. His notion of paradise was a country where individuals worked as they were able, and everyone shared prosperity.

If the government controlled the economy and the people gave their property to the state, no one group of people could ascend over another. Marx defined this ideal in his Manifesto, but the actuality of communism fell well short of the ideal. For a considerable period of the 20th century, roughly one-third of the globe lived in communist countries—countries governed by totalitarian leaders who controlled the lives of everyone else. The communist bosses fixed the salaries, they set the prices, and they divided the riches. Western capitalist nations battled hard against communism, and finally, most communist countries crumbled. Marx's utopia (ideal and perfect society) was never reached since it needed revolution on a worldwide scale, which never came to pass.

Key Principles

While the most commonly known communist nations, such as the Soviet Union, China, and Yugoslavia, established their models which diverged from one other over time, six fundamental traits of pure communist ideology are generally identified.

Collective ownership of the means of production: All means of production such as factories, farms, land, mining, transportation, and communication networks are owned and managed by the state.

Private Property Abolishment: As communal ownership indicates, private ownership of means of production is outlawed. In a strictly communist society, individual residents are permitted to possess nothing save the essentials of existence. The functioning of privately held firms is similarly forbidden.

Democratic centralism: The official organizational and decision-making philosophy of Communist Parties, democratic centralism is a practice in which political decisions, although determined by a supposedly democratic voting procedure, are obligatory on all members of the party—effectively all citizens. As envisaged by Lenin, democratic centralism enables party members to engage in political debate and declare views but requires them to follow the Communist Party "line" after a decision has been reached.

Economy that is centrally planned: Also known as a command economy, a centrally planned economy is an economic system in which a single central authority, often the government in communist governments, controls all decisions about the manufacture and the distribution of goods. Centrally planned economies are distinct from free-market economies, such as those in capitalist nations, in which such choices are made by firms and consumers according to the forces of supply and demand.

Elimination of income inequality: In principle, by rewarding each person according to their need, disparities in income are eliminated. By eradicating revenue, interest income, profit, income disparity, and socioeconomic class friction is abolished, and the distribution of wealth is done on an equitable and fair basis.

Repression: In accord with the idea of democratic centralism, political opposition and economic freedom are outlawed or suppressed. Other essential individual rights and liberties may also be restricted. Historically, communist governments, such as the Soviet Union, were defined by government control of most areas of life. "Correct thinking" in conformity with the party line was pushed via forceful, even frightening propaganda provided by state-owned and controlled media.

Chapter 2: Effects of communism on the society

According to the Marxist theory, the state is by no means the organized power of the community, it is the organized power of the dominant class– specifically, the class holding the principal means of production. Its objective is not universal welfare, but aiding the strong rivals to enhance their riches and power by exploiting the weak competitors as well as the dependent class. In a class-divided society, the individual may have no political commitment toward the state. A person may have a political duty toward society, provided there is a classless and stateless society. Till such a society comes into reality, we can only consider workers' responsibilities toward the working class. Under the capitalist system, when Encinias of the working class is in power, the worker has responsibility against the state'. It demands him to demonstrate unity with the working class to form a powerful organization for revolution against the capitalist dictatorship.

Advantages of communism
Following are the advantages of communism:

- There is less volatility in the economy since the economy is centrally managed.
- The government can perform more effectively because it overrides the individual welfare and works for shared public benefit. For example, USSR readied its army power to destroy the Nazi regime and then swiftly rebuilt for World War II.
- There is a promotion of overall wellbeing.
- Political stability is present because of one part and one ideology.

- Efficiency in the control of government is an example of the success of the Bolshevik regime.
- It is an excellent instrument for mobilizing.

Disadvantages of communism

Theoretically, this theory may be seen as a perfect kind of political philosophy but actually, it involves several disadvantages. Some of them are as follows:

- It encourages people to become lazy because it thinks that trade unions should be there and no private role is there which in return encourages people not to work because they know that they will be paid whether they work or not with the assistance of trade unions.
- There is no pressure or desire to perform more work in comparison with others.

- Due to the creation of trade unions, people are not driven to perform a job and acquire an attitude to receive payment without working.
- There is no innovation as it is against the competition.
- The present is no growth in the country since competition is not there and there is no incentive to achieve better than other countries.
- It fosters smuggling since the people are pleased with what they are creating and are not pushing beyond the point which finally leads to smuggling of the products which can't be produced in the country. This offers invites to various illicit activities like black marketing, smuggling, etc which causes loss to the government and ruins the economy of the country.

Chapter 3: Failures of communism and why it cannot be explained

How could a notion of emancipation lead to so much injustice, tyranny, and death? Were its failings essential to the communist idea, or did they emerge from preventable weaknesses of certain rulers or nations? Like any significant historical development, the shortcomings of communism cannot be reduced to any one particular source. But, by and large, they were truly innate.

Two primary reasons were the most essential causes of the atrocities committed by communist regimes: perverse incentives and insufficient information. The construction of the centrally planned economy and society demanded by socialist ideology entailed an immense concentration of authority. While communists looked forward to a utopian society in which the state might ultimately "wither away," they felt they first had to construct a state-run economy to oversee production in the interests of the people. In that aspect, they had much in common with other socialists.

To make socialism function, government planners are required to have the power to oversee the production and distribution of nearly all the products generated by the community. In addition, substantial pressure was necessary to compel individuals to give up their private property and undertake the tasks that the state demanded. Famine and mass murder was probably the only way the rulers of the USSR, China, and other communist states could compel peasants to give up their land and livestock and accept a new form of serfdom on collective farms – which most were then forbidden to leave without official permission, for fear that they might otherwise seek an easier life elsewhere.

The tremendous authority required to develop and sustain the communist system inevitably attracted dishonest individuals, including many self-seekers who placed their interests above those of the cause. But, notably, the largest communist crimes were performed not by corrupt party executives, but by real believers like Lenin, Stalin, and Mao. Precisely because they were ardent believers, they were prepared to do whatever it may take to make their utopian ideas a reality.

Even while the communist system opened chances for huge crimes by the authorities, it also eliminated productivity incentives for regular people. In the absence of markets (at least legal ones), there was no motivation for employees to either be productive or to concentrate on manufacturing items that may be helpful to customers. Many individuals sought to perform as little work as possible at their official occupations if feasible saving their true efforts for black market activities. As the old Soviet proverb goes, laborers held the mindset that "we pretend to work, and they pretend to pay."

Even when socialist planners desired to generate wealth and match consumer needs, they frequently lacked the knowledge to do so. As Nobel Prize-winning economist F.A. Hayek stated in a renowned piece, a market economy provides crucial information to producers and consumers alike via the pricing system. Market pricing allows producers to recognize the relative worth of various commodities and services, and assess how much customers value their offerings. Under socialist central planning, by contrast, there is no alternative for this crucial expertise. As a consequence, communist planners frequently had no means to determine what to create, by what techniques, or in how amounts. This is one of the reasons why communist regimes constantly suffered from shortages of essential supplies, while concurrently creating enormous amounts of inferior things for which there was little demand.

To this day, proponents of socialist central planning claim that communism failed for preventable situational causes, rather than ones essential to the character of the system. Perhaps the most frequent assertion of this type is that a planned economy can operate effectively so long as it is democratic. The Soviet Union and other communist republics were all dictatorships. But if they had been democratic, maybe the leaders would have had more incentives to make the system function for the benefit of the people. If they failed to do so, the people may "throw the bastards out" in the next election.

Unfortunately, it is improbable that a communist state could stay democratic for long, even if began off that way. Democracy needs competent opposition parties. And to operate, such parties need to be able to send out their message and motivate people, which in turn demands substantial resources. In an economic system in which all or virtually all important resources are owned by the state, the incumbent government may easily suffocate opposition by denying them access to those resources. Under socialism, the opposition cannot operate if they are not permitted to convey their message via state-owned media or utilize state-owned land for their demonstrations and meetings. It is no surprise that practically every communist state repressed opposition groups immediately after coming to power.

Even if a communist state could somehow stay democratic over the long term, it is hard to see how it could handle the twin challenges of knowledge and incentives. Whether democratic or not, a socialist economy would nonetheless involve a massive concentration of power, and substantial coercion. And democratic socialist planners would run into essentially the same information issues as their authoritarian counterparts. In addition, in a society where the government controls all or most of the economy, it would be almost hard for voters to acquire enough expertise to supervise the state's various operations. This will considerably increase the already grave issue of voter illiteracy that plagues contemporary democracy.

Another plausible argument for the failings of communism is that the issue was poor leadership. If only communist nations were not governed by monsters like Stalin or Mao, they may have done better. There is little question that communist nations had more than their share of nasty and even psychopathic leaders. But it is doubtful that this was the key cause of their downfall. Very comparable effects happened in communist countries with leaders who had a broad spectrum of personalities. In the Soviet Union, it is vital to recall that the principal institutions of repression (including the Gulags and the secret police) were formed not by Stalin, but by Vladimir Lenin, a considerably more "normal" person. After Lenin's death, Stalin's chief challenger for power – Leon Trotsky – supported measures that were in some aspects even more draconian than Stalin's own. It's impossible to resist the conclusion that either the personality of the leader was not the key influence, or – alternatively – communist governments tended to elevate bad individuals to positions of authority. Or possibly some of both.

It is also difficult to trust statements that communism failed merely because of faults in the culture of the nations that embraced it. It is true that Russia, the first communist country, has a lengthy history of corruption, authoritarianism, and tyranny. But it is also true that the communists engaged in tyranny and mass murder on a considerably higher scale than in previous Russian administrations. And communism also failed in many other countries with quite different cultures. In the situations of Korea, China, and Germany, individuals with very similar basic cultural roots faced severe poverty under communism but were considerably more successful under market economies.

Overall, the atrocities and failures of communism were the natural outcomes of an effort to establish a socialist economy in which all or nearly all production is controlled by the state. If not always entirely inescapable, the subsequent tyranny was at least extremely plausible.

Just as the horrors of Nazism are terrible lessons on the hazards of nationalism, racism, and antisemitism, so the history of communist crimes illustrates the risks of socialism. The history of communism does not imply that any type of government interference in the economy must be avoided. But it does underscore the perils of enabling the state to gain control of all or most of the economy, and of abolishing private property. Moreover, the information and incentive difficulties that occur under socialism equally bedevil attempts at large-scale economic planning that fall short of total government control of industry.

Sadly, these lessons remain pertinent today, in a period when socialism has again started to draw believers in many areas of the globe. In Venezuela, the government is aiming to construct a new socialist dictatorship that follows much of the same practices as the old, including even the exploitation of food shortages to crush dissent. Even in several long-established democracies, current economic and social crises have bolstered the support of avowed old-style socialists such as Bernie Sanders in the United States and Jeremy Corbyn in Britain. Both Sanders and Corbyn are lifelong advocates of violent communist regimes. Even if they desired to do so, it seems improbable that Sanders or

Corbyn would be able to implement full-blown socialism in their respective nations. But they may wreak enormous harm anyway.

On the opposite side of the political spectrum, there are troubling parallels between communism and other increasingly popular radical right-wing nationalist organizations. Both combine authoritarian impulses with scorn for liberal principles and a determination to increase government control over vast sectors of the economy.

Today's hazardous inclinations on both right and left are not yet as scary as those of a century ago, and need not inflict anywhere like as much damage. The better we absorb the hard lessons of the history of communism, the more probable that we can prevent any replay of its atrocities.

Chapter 4: Why communism should not be encouraged

Even as pure Marxist communism presented the potential for human rights crimes by authoritarian regimes, experts have found two fundamental variables that led to its eventual downfall.

First, under complete communism, the inhabitants have no motive to produce for a profit. In capitalistic cultures, the desire to create for-profit encourages competition and innovation. In communist countries, however, "ideal" people are supposed to selflessly dedicate themselves completely to social goals without regard to personal wellbeing. As Liu Shaoqi, the first Vice-Chairman of the Communist Party of China remarked in 1984, "At all times and all issues a party member should give first attention to the interests of the Party as a whole and put them in the forefront and place personal problems and interests second."

In the Soviet Union, for example, in the absence of free legal markets, employees had little motivation to either be productive or to concentrate on manufacturing items that may be valuable to customers. As consequence, many people sought to perform as little labor as possible on their official government-assigned employment, dedicating their genuine effort to more lucrative black market activities. As many Soviet employees used to remark about their connection with the government, "We pretend to work for them, and they pretend to pay us."

The second reason for the failure of communism was its inherent inefficiencies. For example, the overly complex centralized planning system required the collection and analysis of enormous amounts of detailed economic data. In many situations, this data was error-prone and modified by party-chosen economic planners to create an image of progress. Placing so much power in the hands of so few, fostered inefficiency and corruption. Corruption, sloth, and intensive government monitoring provided little motivation for diligent and hard-working individuals. As a consequence, the centrally planned economy faltered, leaving the people destitute, disillusioned, and unhappy with the communist government.

Conclusion

Not many nations are following communist rule due to its shortcomings like little competition and innovation. The nations that are following the communist system are found to be transitioning from the communist model to other forms of government in reality however on the other side of the coin there are numerous benefits ranging from development to stability of the government.

www.ingramcontent.com/pod-product-compliance
Lightning Source LLC
Chambersburg PA
CBHW071504150726

48000CB00006B/2692